BOOM BOX

Sundress Publications • Knoxville, TN

Editor: Erin Elizabeth Smith
Editorial Assistant: Anna Black

Special thanks to Jenna Jankowski, Stephanie Marker, and Athena
Lathos.

Colophon: This book is set in Adobe Garamond Pro.

Cover Design: Kristen Ton

Book Design: Erin Elizabeth Smith

BOOM BOX

Amorak Huey

Thank you to Maggie Smith for your thoughtful, generous feedback on a draft of this collection. Thanks, as ever, to Chris Haven and the rest of the Poet's Choice club: W. Todd Kaneko, Amy McInnis, Aaron Brossiet, Dean Rader, Brian Clements, Christina Olson, Jean Prokott, Brian Komei Dempster, Judy Halebsky, and Ashley Cardona; you inspire me every month, and this book would not exist without your influence. Thank you to my colleagues in the Grand Valley State University Writing Department for your support. Thank you to Erin Elizabeth Smith for your keen editorial eye and to everyone at Sundress for believing in the poems. For Malcolm, Marilyn, and Silas, there from the start. Finally, always, and most of all, thank you to Ellen, Zoe-Kate, and Eli.

This book was completed with the assistance of a fellowship from the National Endowment for the Arts.

TABLE OF CONTENTS

ONE

TWO

For Mark and Joe —
the boys in the parking lot

ONE

I Have Harnessed Myself Ridiculously to a House
Three Miles Outside a Small Town in Alabama

Place is a kind of truth as walnut trees are a kind of tall.
As persimmon tree, crepe myrtle, chert driveway.
Sharp edges, bitter flesh, a child—me—sliding forward
over the head of a pony. The cold water, the blackened eye.

From this crumbling porch, I can sit on an overturned bucket
and watch the sky turn kudzu-green. Watch the tornado approach.

I can sit a long time without hunger.
There is no one here to count me present.

I am so far gone. I am wearing only the river
which is across the browning field. There are so many churches
within shouting distance, walking distance,
so many kinds of distance. Someday this place

will burn. Become a flat spot where grass will not grow.

Rescue

I should think of it as extraordinary,
this memory of a golden eagle in a cardboard box

in the back room of our house—
its presence a gift,

a wing splintered then splinted.
Sometimes flight is a choice,

there are many ways to heal.
I should go back. As a sort of dawn

filtered over my parents' divorce
my father sidestepped into a new life

and my mother followed her own rope
to find work rehabilitating

injured birds of prey.
There are many ways

to pronounce *beautiful*,
many ways to measure time:

some bones light enough
to be swept away in the wind,

some mornings we woke
in my father's twilit trailer, bored

enough to assassinate beer cans
with firecrackers: make-believe damage.

Every meal needed more salt. *At home*
did not always mean *at home*.

My mother's freezer filled with rat corpses—
sustenance for owls.

The kitchen's yellow tile floor cracked.
Bones mend, though sometimes crooked.

Blood scabs, falls away.
There are many ways this can end.

I should think of all this as extraordinary
but we are not taught to envy the small familiarities

of our own lives. Memory bleeds
into the healing body, past tense

dissolves. What we work toward
is release. A letting go

that begins with a drive to a winter-brown field
we've never seen, will never see again,

our hands in thick gloves. The nearby rivers,
the reaching pines, the open lid of a box.

The wavelike cadence
of a bird transcribing its freedom

in slowly widening circles:
the looping back,

the looping back.
So many paths, so much to leave behind.

Portrait of My Father as Tatooine

A man with two sons sometimes forgets
the shape of flame. Sometimes forgets
to warn of the danger of downed wires.
He struggles to describe loneliness,
to know how much he should reveal
about how the ground has shifted,
was always shifting. He knows
there are adventures and there are movies
about adventures. There are Saturdays
and the idea of Saturdays.
He is always remembering advice
he should have given—how to extinguish
a campfire, never to spit into the wind,
why a triangle is the strongest shape,
how to keep fingers away from blade,
never to shoot an arrow straight up into the air.
He sees himself in his sons but does not recognize
the sound of broken glass. These are not
the days he was looking for.
The world arranges itself into visits
and the space between: a dry lakebed at dusk,
the crushed, papery skull of a heron,
a burned spot in the sand—
the man's fears made tangible,
his dreams all of the same thirsty planet.

All Weather Wants to Be Some Other Kind of Weather

A boy lies on top of his sheets in Alabama,
his skin glazed with sweat and wonder.
The late-summer air is soup, swamp,
tongue. The boy suspects he was kidnapped
as an infant. Suspects he does not belong,
here or anywhere, has no home to return to,
and if once he had some other name
it has long been forgotten. The darkness
is a promise. The quiet is a promise.
He opens his eyes. Closes them.
And for the rest of his life
he will pretend there was a time
when he was comfortable in his skin—
a season that was not about waiting
for the wind to change—
a moment unshaped by hunger.

Portrait of My Brother as Indiana Jones

Barbed-wire fence. Pasture. Stand of water oaks.
This was the path to the river. Sometimes chased,
sometimes chasing, always moving fast,
sometimes an enormous rolling rock,
sometimes a hail of spears and arrows,
afraid of nothing more than standing still.
All a young man has is his faith in hard work,
the belief that if only he can count
the grains of sand in a fist-sized sack,
things will turn out as he hopes—
that when he returns home
there will be quiet afternoons
and a girl in a sweater with love on her eyelids—
yet every adventure ends
in the same weary surprise,
the same aching temples
when the poison darts fly,
when the floor drops from beneath,
when fatherhood looms and the bills come due,
when vision closes in from the corners,
when the dark mass requires surgery,
when they cut open his skull
because the only threats that matter
were inside all along.

Dead Man's Float

Late summer, Cahaba River, practicing buoyancy.
I am young enough to expect I will survive.

Hold breath like pebble in mouth, testing self. Muted warble,
underwater rush. Taste of salt. Shine and sweep of river's bottom—

this oblong distortion. Somewhere, my parents stall and smear
and cheapen the inevitable. We watch and watch,

intuition kindled in argument. The world flattens
as we grow up: drone of adulthood: shaking, colorless future.

Pressure swells, defusing trance. Surprising how easy
to imagine surroundings after so much time without looking:

blackened foliage, fallen nests, splintered stumps.
Listen carefully for the thorns. Something inside breaks loose.

Lift face from surface. It is morning. Everything is visible.

The Skies Above the Little League Fields of My Memory

are green and ripe: tornado weather. These fields
are lush, vast, impossible, populated
by fathers and sons and the things that step between us.
These fields are where we learn to fall in love,
learn not to tell anyone when a fastball leaves a mark.
They have the wet-penny smell of leather and neatsfoot oil,
the roar of nearby lawnmowers and disapproval.
They are flanked by cinder-block dugouts,
used condoms and cigarette butts turning to dust
in gravel parking lots, overflowing toilets in the bathrooms—
these are the fields where we learn position and stance,
learn to dig in our feet and stride toward what we want to hit.
We order suicides from the concession stand:
every drink they have and the taste of grape.
The coach named Red and the coach named Pop
argue balls and strikes and the politics of All-Star teams,
fathers arrive to help us practice in their ties and shiny shoes,
in their workboots and bruised knuckles.
It's all posture and performance, a slow parade
through a small town, last season's champions
waving from atop a glistening fire engine.

Seven Postcards from Trussville, Alabama

1.
A field in the slanting sun past the north end of town—
dappled light, distant highway.
The dead grass. The ringing phones.
The missing boy. The missing girl.
The wishing you were here.
The town itself, as if underwater.

2.
An eighth-grade biology class walks to the river
to capture samples of whatever's just passing through.
Honors students, the future in their eyes,
all those somewhere elses,
tenderness in what they do not know.

3.
When the boy was 11, he spent three hours on a Sunday night
flushing gravel down the toilets at the Little League field.
Considerable damage.
An investigation.
A season delayed.

4.
Skin is thinnest on eyelids and lips
and the backs of our hands.
Some people bruise more easily.

5.
Three things you cannot be sure of in Trussville:
    a. Who is listening
    b. From which direction the wind
    c. The secrets to keep, the secrets to spill

6.
The hardware store has everything anyone might need in this world.
Check the back aisles, past the thicknesses of rope
and the barrels of nails. For the next world,
there is a church down the block.
Up the hill, another.
And another.

7.
In a park overlooking the river,
a concrete picnic table disintegrates.

The Fathers at the Little League Field
Trussville, Alabama, 1981

They cluster like bandits in this late-spring breeze,
lean against right field fence with practiced swagger

even in their stillness. The boys before them,
running through the dwindling green hours

and the close-mown chalk-line fields of potential, already
sag invisibly under their fathers' undreamt dreams.

These fathers know what unfolds, what corners,
what cannot be contained by highway, riverbank.

A foul out of play bounds toward parking lot,
one man jingles keys and says too loudly,

Hoo boy, better move that 'Bird, which he does,
giving the engine an unnecessary punch

before shifting into drive for the 200-foot journey
to safer haven. The unwritten ways

we call attention to ourselves render us immortal.
These fathers never had a problem disappointment couldn't solve.

They have witnessed the convergence of time and lack,
they know talent has a ceiling, fidelity

is the last virtue of the passed-by, truth
is for Sunday mornings. Every one of them still

hits like an all-star, fucks like a Hall of Famer.
They complain about wives and bosses,

they pretend to leer at the high school girls
working the concession stand.

It's all almost plausible. One man
passes his flask, they grimace and swig

and swear and feel better about themselves.
Above them, the field lights hum to life,

a million moths clump and whirl and dive.
The game has tightened in the late innings,

the shouting grows tense, important.
Cigarettes are flicked into the gravel,

embers blur to ash. This is when things will be decided.
These men are thirty-three or forty-four,

their ties are loosened, they scuff nicer shoes
than their own fathers ever owned. They sell

and supervise, commute and count and keep score.
There is nothing they can't have.

Everything I Know About Life I Learned from 1980s Action Shows

If convicted of a crime you did not commit,
make sure they let you keep the car you did not steal.
Cars matter in a world that's cherry red, glistening,
has its sleeves shoved to its elbows, sweatless,
eternally cool in the swamp of a Miami summer.
The synthesizer is the most magical of instruments,
is the soundtrack for any mood,
is the salt in the water, bikini in the opening sequence,
powder on the mirror at a glamorous party. You
will never attend parties like this. Every chase
ends in a warehouse, every warehouse
features a backroom that contains the tools and materials
needed to construct a handmade cannon
suitable for launching cabbages through the eye of a tank—
do not lock your enemies in this room
for they are clever and the hour is nearing an end.
Coincidence is an art form. You start
a decade at age ten, end it at twenty
and it's only later you see how little you changed.
Time travel fits in your pocket, sixty minutes
is long enough to rule the world
and even a blank cartridge can kill.
Homicide detectives are rule-breakers
though most of them played in the NFL,
passwords are guessable,
living on a houseboat is a thing adults do
and the sky is full of helicopters.
Fear the mustache. Fear the tiny tiny shorts.
If the guest star has a gold medal it must be sweeps month.
Narrative must work in black and white—
color is a luxury and never lifelike.
There is no problem that can't be contained

in fifteen inches and three acts, no cliffhanger
or commercial that doesn't make you hungry.
All you have to do is show up and watch. Every series
has the soul of a Western, even the president
is made for TV, everyone else in the world
has money, all the names are ridiculous,
the last word is a laugh line.
Sometimes the star is replaced. Sometimes
the whole cast. You pretend not to notice. This is
the covenant you make with each new season
as the cars crash and the neon credits roll—
if Ponch is fungible, we all are.

The Older Brother's Guide to Cheating at Monopoly

The year of the divorce, all springflood and tornado warning,
Cahaba River swollen beyond reason or containment,
Happy Hollow Road washed out and we were trapped:

ten days of our parents barely able to look at each other.
Chores and games were all we had—once the animals were fed
we rolled dice, dealt cards, kept score in too-convenient metaphors:

Life, Careers, Clue, Battleship, Risk. But looking back I find
little narrative, less rhyme scheme
as the lyricism of my parents' love story unraveled,

my brother and I too young to see beyond our own skin,
our hunger for predictability. We didn't have TV until a year later
in our father's apartment so we weren't yet in the thrall

of *The A-Team*, *Knight Rider*, *CHiPs*—every episode
beginning with an implausible car wreck, vehicles in a pile
with no one injured who couldn't be pulled free by Ponch or Jon.

Our heroes lived on baseball cards, everything we needed
to know about their life stories in neat columns of numbers on the back.
It all comes together so obviously, doesn't it? I am older now

than my parents then, with kids of my own who ask only
for every instant of my attention—not one thing more—
so I sense the sacrifice they made when at last

we talked them into joining us for Monopoly.
We bought, sold, bartered, mortgaged, developed, took second prize
in beauty contest after beauty contest. We passed Go,

collected our due, went directly to jail, took rides on the Reading
in this game that refused to end, not even
when the rain stopped and they fixed the road.

My parents had enough, but we would not quit.
Eventually they divided their properties between us,
returned to the dismantling of their marriage,

but my brother and I were committed to see it through.
I'd like to tell you how it ended, to persuade you
the way things turned out meant something about capitalism,

about the nature of human affairs—but I don't recall. I'm sure I won,
appointing myself banker and stacking the deck in my favor,
for which I should now apologize, but to whom? For what?

What I do know: it hardly rained those dusty deadgrass months,
we escaped our house gone silent, built a fort in the woods—
dug a hole ten feet square, four feet deep, covered it with pine boughs,

told no one of its existence. We were working against a deadline,
a season that had stretched endlessly in front of us
growing shorter by the day and so much to learn about architecture.

Land Fall

We are two hundred miles inland but directly in the path and already the sky is heavy and green and the rain tastes of salt. Our driveway is underwater. The goats are restless, bleating. The chickens huddle. Earlier, our parents lost patience with each other and my father took the truck. The lights are flickering, the power wavering. Each passed hour becomes a link in the chain of an uncertain narrative. In other words: the ending has not been written. Will not be written today, unless it is. The wind brings the smell of the sea and scraps of trash that tap and jazz across the yard. The lightning draws nearer, the thunder grows louder, like sheets of corrugated tin rattling in the back of a pickup bouncing along a long dirt road. We were born for weather like this—a storm we might survive but will not escape.

Cigarette vs. Cookie

My mother is leaving. My father is leaving.
We are all leaving, that's the only truth. Someone
rhymes their fists against the hood of a rusted white pickup:

knuckle-bruise and raised-voice—am I in the truck?
Am I on the porch, watching the tires crescendo gravel
as what's left of the morning fishtails out of our driveway?

I will remember it both ways—as the one leaving,
as the one left behind, as if there's a difference.
As if I'm not already inventing the details:

all these roles, more than enough for each of us.
My mother smokes. My father smokes.
We are a family of tiny fires and empty bottles.

We are a study in the high cost of being in a hurry, lessons
we learn and relearn. The horse trailer loose and rattling behind.
The horse trailer wrenching free at the end of the drive,

tilting into our tallest oak tree with a noise like a stepped-on beer can,
sometimes we have no choice but to stop and start over.
We are in awe of this tree, its testament to standing still,

to time and the luck that carries lightning somewhere else.
I'm listening to "Harper Valley PTA" or "Ode to Billie Joe"
and imagining some other life. I'm eating the last of the Tagalongs

and watching my parents reattach the trailer. So much
swearing. So many smoke breaks. It's my pony
we have to pick up from the vet. There is no work

without blame. We have each other's full attention now.
I'm asking who would win if cigarette fought cookie.
Why would they fight? To see how sugar tastes when it burns.

Happy Hollow Road, 1960-1979: A History in Six Voices

I am spray-painting "pussy" on a rusted bridge girder.
I am lost, turning left and left behind. I'm bow-hunting
squirrel with my father in the rain. I married
into every generation of this family. The dirt track
twists uphill: gear down, spew gravel, accelerate hard—
around the last curve, a sand pit where I break down
stolen muscle cars into sellable parts:
American heavy metal and whatever brings in a dollar.
I am forest fire, Gillespie's pasture, Cahaba River.
I am water oak, cedar, long-needle pine. I park
behind Mount Olive Baptist with the girls of my dreams,
we tongue and twist and tell stories about tomorrow.
I moved here young. I raise bantams,
all bluster and tailfeathers, and Saturday nights
are for killing. My sons go to war. Some return,
changed. The interstate noise is still new enough
to be surprising every night. I am innocent
but the accusation has the ring of truth.
It's home. It's the spring floods—the danger
of fast water, the cleansing. We throw our trash
in a ditch behind the barn. We don't apologize.
We take care of our own. It's a nice thing to say.
We build houses on the corners of our parents' property,
we pass Mason jars of homebrewed moonshine
around bonfires, burning leaves. Our flags
do not mean what you think they mean.
Yes, there are guns, and sometimes they go off—
it's a narrative requirement. Every stone
in every graveyard had to be dug up somewhere.
Follow the curve, the fork, the new growth.
The world is coming, though we don't see it yet.
Stay for supper and don't you dare
condescend to me. I drive home

with a Pabst between my thighs
and the past on my mind. Mostly I arrive
without incident. I chase the kids next door
with a BB gun and ask my Ouija board
questions about sex. The old mill
sags and splinters and slips into the river.
We are north of Trussville, south of Springville,
we have lived here since the dawn of time,
in this place between other places.
In the woods behind our house, a granite boulder
the size of a school bus where we scattered
my grandmother's ashes. Somewhere else
in the woods, an abandoned shed:
broken window, rusted nails, a box of skin mags.
Fuck you if you can't take a joke or keep a secret.
Every No Trespassing sign pockmarked
from shotgun spray. Every tree choked
with climbing kudzu. Every one of us in love
with someone untouchable—we are bodies
at rest, bodies in motion. This is no one's shortcut.

Self-Portrait as Dustin Hoffman in *Tootsie*

Divorce unshapes our family into a set of occasionally intersecting lines. It means more movies, more swearing, more time in cars. Transitions are shaped like doorknobs. For the first time, hours are countable. I learn early the importance of ritual and mask, the way silence falls from the light slicing through the darkness over our heads, a wedge widening until it reaches the blank screen and becomes someone else's adventure story. I am too young for any of this. The world isn't waiting for me to be the right age. I whisper profanity but no one hears me. I speak with a New York accent for the entire year I am twelve. I am waiting for my life to include an apartment, a roommate, a party on the roof of a building made of glass and sex and alcohol. Maybe cigarettes. I will wear whatever you ask me to, but it never was about the shimmering dress, the eyeliner, the foundation. It was always about Jessica Lange's mouth and how the life you deserve is worth lying for.

The Existence of Han Solo Explains the Universe

1.
It is 1977 and I am seven and seven is everyone's lucky number.
I have never been able to turn a cartwheel—my mistake

is expecting this will change—expecting I will grow
into the spin and whirl, the placing of hands on solid ground

then the letting go of this earth, the seeing what happens next.

2.
In ascending order: jackknife, Hot Wheels Porsche, plastic M-16,
library books, first baseman's mitt, cassette deck, Han Solo.

3.
Anything I offer about the stars over Alabama in the 1970s
will sound made up, the trick of a fickle memory.

The sky turns green and tangible during tornado season, leaving
the world underwater and my parents arguing
over whether to go to the grand opening of the Handy Dan.

We color stars white but in truth they are blue or pink,
light bending across the impossible arc of distance and time

and what appears black is only the limit of our field of vision—
we believe we want to be the hero but in truth

knowing what we want has never been our strength.

4.
Han Solo is no one's savior. Han Solo
shoots first. And last. Han Solo
has a keen sense of what's impossible.
Han Solo has a ship full of money

and his unrequited love to keep him company.
The movie gets it all wrong
and the sequels are someone else's dreams—
there's a limit to how much truth we can stand.

5.
What we think of as beauty is, in fact, dust.
Imagine the slamming of a screen door. The ache
in the back of the throat that stands for yearning.
Imagine the rules changing. And changing.
Imagine not being told the rules in the first place—
if I could return, would I? What would be

different? In all my memories of my parents
they are in separate rooms. Yet I know
this is invented. I've gotten it wrong,

and still am. The fire starts. How bright the ice that burns.

6.
Han Solo does not need an origin story.
Han Solo does not need your religion,
your narrative rules, your rhyme.

Han Solo is peacock and pose,
blast and swagger, skinny legs
and a mouthful of galaxies.

Han Solo is black hole swallowing,
Death Star exploding,
star winking out—the light, the absence.

Han Solo has never been captured—
carbonite is an illusion. Han Solo
is and is and simply is.

7.
My father is not Han Solo.
I am not Han Solo.
What's misleading

about movies
is the ending is obvious—

ratcheta-ratcheta-ratcheta
of film slapping against projector,
motes suddenly visible

in a horizontal shaft of light.

8.
It is 2013 and my tolerance for standing in line
has dwindled to nothing.
Han Solo lives across the street from me now,

neighbor but nothing like neighborly,
house in foreclosure, yard overgrown,
we see him buying wine

in his black vest and plaid pajama pants,
wife gone, girlfriend gone,
he yells at our children,

he is a cartoon character, bloated and sad
and full of anger. We peer
in his front window: a hallway full

of garbage, a radio on too loud all night,
receiving signals from somewhere
and spitting them out.

Self-Portrait Following a Trail of Reese's Pieces

I am never sure whether I am the alien lost far from home or the kid who befriends the alien. This is the year I learn protagonist and sidekick are not always properly labeled, the year filled with Marlboro smoke and divorce, the year I refuse to tie my shoes. I wait for my body to betray me, to announce my hunger to a disapproving world. Until it reaches the screen and turns back toward the audience, a movie is only moonlight and soundtrack. Light is invisible but without it so is everything else, and maybe this moment is not my life but the reflection of my life. "Penis breath" is the best insult ever written, it's exactly what we waited in line for. In the dark, no one sees how uncomfortable I am in this body.

Dungeon Master's Guide to Eighth Grade

"As long as your campaign remains viable,
it will continue a slow process of change and growth."
—Gary Gygax

When you come back in the fall of 1983
your friends listen to Z-103 instead of KIX-106,
Luke Skywalker isn't cool anymore
and they might still watch *The A-Team*
but no one talks about it. Will you search each room
or move on quickly? Roll for traps. Boys swear
like their uncles. Armpit hair is a status symbol.
The lunchroom is an unguarded wilderness
of potential humiliation. So is conversation.
This is when *every* girl is out of your league,
when you realize such leagues even exist.
It's Panama Jack shirts and parachute pants,
it's when neatness begins to count
in algebra and Earth science
and how you part your hair. It's when art
is no longer for everyone. When size matters.
Roll for attributes. Choose alignments.
Every outcome will matter forever.
The halls smell like hairspray and belch.
The Cold War heats up, there are drills
for when the Russians attack—basically, duck.
This is when curve balls actually curve,
the kid who used to play short is in right,
the kid who played right field is in the band,
some new kid the star of every team.
The answers are all behind the screen.
You stop mentioning your interests,
start planning evasive action
to survive from homeroom to history.
Life happens one period at a time. It's turn-based

and someone else's move. Roll
and roll again. Each day's final bell
is a tally mark scratched into painted cinderblock.
The world is populated with non-player characters.
Later you'll see there's always a Cold War somewhere.
Not every dragon lives in a dungeon.
The last to realize this dies first.

How to Set a Fire and Why

Twisted Sister changes everything.
Bony T's and S's interlock
in ballpoint blue from the back row
of a life, filling what's empty
in my notebooks. It seems
so obvious, giving music
to hunger. My first sound
cried *feed me*, like anyone's,
but my first word was *hot*
and you asked about the fire,
how we arrive at ash. Easy:
press play. Wish for lightning.

You Are *Never* Too Big to Open for KISS

My friends knew more about God than I did,
and more about KISS:

the solo albums, the apostles,
old drummer and New Testament,

for every kind of gospel
there's a clumsy metaphor for desire;

we all need something to do with our tongues
while we wait for salvation.

We've got things all out of proportion,
honestly, it's an issue for the species—

when Sebastian Bach scored Skid Row a gig
opening for KISS, his bandmates fired him.

Ever Since the Movies Taught Me About
the Space-Time Continuum

I have begun to see my body as gap, absence, rending:
the hole between a moment
and the more meaningful moment that follows.

Between, say, calling to request "Legs"
and the DJ finally playing the song.

Between my friend's stepfather careening home
and the yelling downstairs.

Between pushing play and the tape beginning to turn.
Between the tape and the sound.

Or the pause between *Oooh, I want her* and *Shit, I got to have her.*
Oh, to sing like that. To be honest about desire.

The broken porch light. The dark driveway. The squealing tires.
We have no idea what we want or how to escape.

My friend is embarrassed by his stepfather's swearing,
by the store-brand cola in the refrigerator, by his own mutable flesh.
My friend doesn't look down when he pees.
My friend has no idea how I feel about his older sister,
her thighs and the Judas Priest concert shirt she wears to bed,
my plans to tap softly on her door

after everyone else falls asleep and before this narrative falls apart
because I have no idea what happens next—

how the time might pass between that moment and the rest of my life.

I have no idea how old I am in this story. In any story.
I will never feel any different than I do right now
but I do not yet know this.

My friend has to get up early
because he goes to church with his mother on Sunday mornings.
Also Sunday nights and Wednesday nights.
This is so much God, you have no idea.

On their way to salvation, they will drop me off at home
because I do not have appropriate clothes.
I will lock myself in my room and catch up on my dreams:
the ripening. The fall. The chasm between.

The Boy Who Believed in the Girl Who Did Not Believe in God

They're supposed to be learning something about Emily Dickinson and "The Yellow Rose of Texas" but no one's sure why it matters. The girl is drawing a butterfly on the soft skin of the inside of the boy's forearm with a blue ballpoint Bic. His mistake is thinking *skin* is the word that matters. His mistake is thinking *ink*, thinking *heartbeat* and *fingertip*. The average lifespan for most species of butterfly is a month, and the girl knows better than to ask for an exception, she knows the season will outlast this restlessness she feels. She knows the boy's desire should not be confused with her own. The lesson is about rhythm—is about faith.

Boom Box

My father leaves again. Returns, falls asleep
in the driveway with a warm six-pack of Pabst
like a fist between his thighs. He swears
he has not been gone that long, is not
that drunk. My mother smokes more now
than before she quit. The fire
was four years ago, we're still living
in a trailer parked behind
the charcoaled foundation of our old house.
Before it's too late I should
mention the rifle, the box of bullets
I found in the back of the closet
behind the skin mags, the vibrator.
My parents don't even talk to each other
but the body is capable of all kinds of lies.
My mother will not let me listen
to Run-DMC, which she says
is because of God but I know better.
All those gold chains, such audacity.
She doesn't know anything about me.
I steal Marlboros one at time,
matches from the back of the stove,
I'm cutting the sleeves out of my t-shirts
these days, freaking out the neighbor kids
by spelling *pussy* on my Ouija board,
trying to make it sound like bragging,
telling them this summer I'm going to get
Stella from up the hill to pull up her shirt for me.
I carry my boom box everywhere,
my secret cassette of *Raising Hell*,
sometimes the gun. I can make
anyone believe anything. Maybe
my father hits me. Maybe the war

changed him, though I never knew him before,
so what do I know? Maybe I shoot
at squirrels but can never hit one.
Maybe I'm hanging out on the girders
of the old bridge with the volume on 10,
hoping one of these songs will piss off someone
enough to stop and give me a talking-to.
Maybe I'm setting fire to sticks
and dropping them in the water.
Maybe I killed one of the coon hounds
caged up by Stella's asshole dad
who maybe hits her sometimes, too,
maybe hurts her in more silent ways.
Maybe I hope she is as lonely as I am.
Maybe this is the most fucked-up time
in the history of the world
to be fourteen, maybe there's some poison
in the river that feeds our wells.
Maybe I can feel my skin blistering
from the inside out, maybe the bruises
are bleeding into each other. What a mess.
Maybe the gun never even goes off.
Maybe it's only the music announcing
I am here. Maybe I'm shouting
my own name, over and over, synced
with the beat. Boom, boom,
like that. Boom.

TWO

Crimes I Did Not Commit

I did not opt early for grief over guilt. I did not
hide under the kitchen table to eavesdrop
on arguing parents. I did not yell the word *divorce*
into my brother's face until he cried
so I could paint my parents with his tears,
anything to speed the arrival of silence.
I did not learn to hate the tractor,
did not pour sugar in the gas tank
because I'd read it would foul the engine
and I was in no mood for chores.
If I did, it did not work. Not everything
we read is telling that kind of truth.
There was no hurricane. No green-black sky
sinking heavy over the hills. I am not
necessary to this story. Without me, then:
boy meets girl, etc. The usual mess
of falling in love against the odds,
and the usual outcome: the odds bear out.
Everything I know about hunger
did not come from sneak-reading
the dirty parts of *Clan of the Cave Bear*.
I did not find skin mags in a shed in the woods.
Did not touch myself for years.
Did not steal a neighbor boy's bike
and shove it off the old bridge
in the spring-swelled Cahaba River.
Did not then help him look for that bike
in every driveway and open garage
for three miles along Happy Hollow Road.
Did not agree when he decided
some black kids must have taken it
though there were no black families
for miles. I am not expecting forgiveness.

I have never been erased from the plot.
Never held a gun. Never climbed to the top
of the rusting girders to stare down
at the quiet water, the murking rocks.
Never imagined I could change the world
by disappearing. I did not pretend
to find God because I did not believe
this would persuade a girl to touch me.
If I did, it did not work. This is not
that kind of story. This is not a confession.
This is a heart growing wings and taking flight,
up above the scrub pine and water oak,
hurrying out ahead of the storm.

Still Life with *Appetite for Destruction* Playing in the Background

A boy walks through a kudzu-green park
holding hands with a girl who is not there.
Every girl he has kissed has been

some kind of Kristi—all eyes and whys
and hard seas. Eventually they disappear

but this is not his fault. Prom night,
Dirty Dancing in the basement,
spring birthdays. Beside him the Cahaba:
muddy, unceasing, certain. Open lips,

impossible hunger, mirror steamed over.

Triangle the strongest shape,
metal the only music worth listening to,
such efficient structures, little effort wasted—
in front of him, a concrete picnic table

set for two. He sits. Waits.

The Elegy Arrives Too Late to Change Anything, Which Is Sort of the Definition of Elegy

Elegy for a boy who no longer exists. Elegy for the girl he loves, or loved once, one late spring or early summer, a season spent in the back seat of her mother's Taurus, a cassette of Cinderella's new album draining the battery and curfew fast approaching. Elegy for the sweetness in how they reach for each other, for the guitar solos collecting in their eyelashes. This is the year the river floods. The river floods every year until the shape of the river is the shape of a flood. He asks her to turn on the dome light because he wants to see her. She says let's take a walk instead. They should already be on their way home, but they are so young and the air is so warm, the water so dark and their footing so uncertain. For a while, you think someone is going to drown, but it's not that kind of elegy.

To All the Boys Who Died Before Graduation

Fuck did we know in 1987?
Only what we'd heard, that's what,

that the Camaro was going nearly 100,
telephone pole immutable and maybe John

was standing up through the moonroof
drinking his share of nightsky,

every conclusion inevitable as third-period algebra—
that maybe Danny overdosed,

Keith fell asleep driving home,
Brad—I think that was his name—

drunk and walking on the railroad tracks
that skirted the western edge of town.

All any of us had in common
was our taste in music—our thirst

for expensive speakers, bass boosters,
amplifiers, equalizers: dashboards

deadly as missile silos, rocket consoles.
We banged our heads, our hearts

and all we knew of love was enough
to rhyme lips and fingertips:

every album had exactly one ballad. We knew
the best place to get lucky with a dance squad girl

was the darkest corner of the hospital parking lot,
we knew the *Lost Boys* soundtrack

would make us look sensitive,
Joshua Tree was for pussies

and seventeen the only age worth being.
We knew the Burger King on Parkway East

was the place to go if you wanted to fight
kids from Huffman or Erwin, we knew

the cops would arrest no one but send us all home,
spilling and sprawling and thumping into our cars

and learning exactly what we wanted to learn.
We knew if you waited long enough

in the parking lot at the ABC Store
someone would take your money and buy your beer.

We were motherfucking immortal and *still*
we knew everything

would be ripped away—not *if* but *when*
we would hear the news before first bell rang,

one kid whispering the name, then another,
so by the time the principal cleared his throat on the intercom

and asked for a moment of silence
we would already have grieved and gone on,

grateful and hungry and burning, always burning.

The Loneliest Boy in Alabama Listens to "Wild Side" and "Girls, Girls, Girls" Over and Over While Driving in Circles Outside the Bama Six

What if there's nothing else?
What if this *is* the poem?

How I Got This Way

Often in the movie version they'll connect the main villain to the hero's origin story even if that's not how it really happened. This is in the interest of a compelling narrative. Like that time Kristi went to church camp over spring break and came back to ask whether I believed in God, and I said yes. She broke up with me anyway because of God, or maybe it was because of the boy across the street, or the boy who got the spot I wanted on the varsity baseball team, I've lost track, but it all works better if this story is about her and not Amy or April or Traci or some other girl I've half-remembered, half-invented. The blood in my mouth hurts more if all the lies are for the same person. Like, does anyone believe that snake in the Garden of Eden is really the same guy from the end times? That's just a trope to help us see how seeds planted early on bear fruit later in the story. See what I did there? I did it for you, the way I went to that church to hear you sing, to watch you worship, to see what shape faith takes when it takes the shape of your body.

What Religion Means to Me

Religion is why
Kristi broke up with me my senior year
　　in Holier-Than-Y'all, Alabama.
All the girls spent spring break at church camp,
　　　　came home and dumped their boyfriends

because of our ungodly desires

or theirs. Kristi ended us, then washed
　　　　my car in her driveway
to pay off a friendly wager
　　　her words had rendered irrelevant
　　　　　and to show she meant me no ill will.

I drove home down the longest country road I knew,
trailing a rooster-tail plume of white dust,
　　　stopping to taste sweet dark wild fruit on the roadside.

I thought I understood something about the path through heartbreak,

how its shoulders were choked with kudzu
and purple-bruised blossoms smelling of homemade grape wine.
　　　My friends all worshiped
at the First Church of Our Steeple Is Taller Than The Methodists'

and once after I visited, three men came to witness to my family
　　　and tell my mother they were sorry
she didn't care about her children
　　　　as she didn't send us to church.

My twelfth-grade English teacher told us
　　　which translations of the Bible would get us to heaven.
　　　　The vice principal argued theology

with Robyn, the only out-and-proud atheist I knew,

who wore her faithlessness like a gaudy blouse with shoes to match.

        Mr. Carter thought to trump her by asking:
       How can a brown cow eat green grass and make white milk
if not by the hand of God?

The worst part is, when Kristi sat me down and asked
         was I a Christian
I looked deep into her tawny lion-eyes and by god I lied.

      Purer, simpler faith has never existed

than mine at that moment, nor any martyr felt more forsaken
          than when she said she was breaking things off anyway
       though she was happy to know I, too, would be in heaven.

I withstood this test. I still believe
      religion is
the pale taste of sweat on the skin of the breast of the woman I adore,

stain of blackberries on the fingers,
      hot whisper against the throat—a prayer

        to be loved that only the devout can hear.

In Praise of Charlotte Giattina's 1988 Monte Carlo SS

Each season we scrap new cars and wars and women,
we sense early the value of fast and untouchable.
Heat lightning fills our horizons, that searing
impossible love our favorite songs know all about.

We learn early to brag about fast girls, untouchable cars:
Trans Am, Camaro, Mustang, Firebird, we have wings
and nothing is impossible, not even love, though we know nothing,
we start over each night as flat as prom photos, airbrushed tattoos

and Trans Am T-shirts, all horsepower and eagle wings,
so much swagger and shimmy and skinny hips, we are peacocks
in airbrushed yearbook photos, we tattoo each other's names
on unseen skin. The lines we draw kick up dust

as we swagger and shimmy down skinny backroads, peacocks
and rooster tails, working up the nerve to hold hands,
fingertips touching unseen skin, color outside the lines, dust
to lust, ashes to crashes—unrequited violence,

iridescent rooster-crow confidence we hold in our hands.
All these girls, their lips and graduation gifts: MR2s, Fieros, Preludes:
our lust grows up fast and crashes with gleeful violence
into the revved-up bric-a-brac of being eighteen—

these girls, their fire-breathing: no way to know what's prelude,
what's final act when each season brings new cars and wars and women.
We are consumed by acceleration, the flotsam of being young—
we are blinded by this heat lightning. This searing.

The Boys in the Parking Lot

I don't know how we did any of it: that sleepless, swaggering summer

soundtracked by drum solo, rhythm guitar,
our names tattooed in intricate snakes and skulls

across our movie-version visions of ourselves. So hot that year
the blacktop still sticky at midnight,

we angled our cars just so, and our bodies—
every move a pose,

every pause an image
that might be our first album cover—

the intense one, the sad one, the bored one

each staring into the middle distance
as if any of us could see anything
outside of our own skin.

Elegy for *Dirty Dancing*

There are planets that could sustain life
but that doesn't mean they do.
There are parts of this world
where humidity is the meaning of life.
It's the water. The possibility of water.
Flesh. The possibility of flesh.
Seventeen was a dark and hungry age
when any irony I could muster
was directed outward—when I could still imagine
growing up to be tough but tender,
a strong-armed loverboy, dancer, brawler.
When I could pretend to love
a movie or pretend to hate it, whatever
got me to the carpet in someone's basement,
the VCR rewinding, her parents asleep upstairs
and the clock ticking toward curfew.
It's hard to figure out who you are
when all you want is definition
in your biceps and someone to notice.
Every month was August in the South those days,
the air tangible, malleable, every secret
exposed, all swelter and sweat and the quiet music
of a river learning to love its banks all over again,
a virgin learning to dance like a movie star—
the rushing past, the holding on.

Ouroboros, Alabama

The town eventually swallowed itself and doubled in size. On the highway toward the next town was a fire-extinguisher factory; now they make small children there. The children grow up and breed. It's all very self-contained. The ice cream stand closed and became a different ice cream stand, which also closed. Once we had a barbecue joint we all liked, but no one ate there. It was red and shaped like the hole a barn would leave if it ran through a wall and left a hole shaped like a barn. The sign promised "Open for Breakfast," but that was a long time ago. Every year someone young died trying to cross the tracks before the train came. The trains were only four or five cars long, but young people are in such a hurry. Some of us drowned instead, after drinking wine coolers down by the baseball fields and forgetting about the river, the old bridge. "Beats dying of a broken heart," the survivors would say. If it sounds like we didn't care, it's only because you haven't seen us in our church clothes. Most of us stuck around, but some of us left and send postcards with cryptic messages and pictures that imply we are somewhere sexy. We are careful not to say "Wish you were here," because that's the opposite of what anyone wishes.

There Is No Other Devil Anymore

So the preacher goes after our music.
He's posturing for what he believes,

thinks he's pandering to a friendly crowd—
Hello, First Baptist! and so forth—

our parents nodding in time,
wary of their daughters' growing appetites

and the length of their sons' hair
until he calls out "Bridge over Troubled Water"

as Satan's hymn to heroin.
At this point even the old folks tune out, a chord

too close to home. Of course
he's right about music making us hungry,

though we may disagree on the wages of hunger.
What's the joke? If you want someone

to drink all your booze, invite a Baptist to dinner.
If you don't want your liquor touched, invite two.

This is America. This is Alabama.
We are all headbangers in this church

built of the bones of the past and rooted in red dirt.
It's 1980-something, I am present at this sermon

for the best of all reasons: to convince a girl
I am worthy of her glance. I am not.

I know nothing about salvation,
though I pretend otherwise.

The only injustices I've tasted are personal,
invented, and if she would only

turn her eyes this way, I would show her
what I understand about blind faith. To my surprise

I feel a kinship with the preacher—
his clumsy attempt to save

himself from the world
and the world from all our weakness

has fallen short by exactly the distance
between a body and a belief.

Self-Portrait as C.C. DeVille Auditioning for Poison

Stop me if you've heard this one: scorpion
          promises not to sting frog,
frog agrees to provide a lift over flooded river.

The storms I imagine strut across the sky,

thread guitar strings through oak limbs,
          rip off your clothes,
leave you strewn across river's edge

as the water rises. It's all fantasy I'm selling,
mostly what I do is wait out the rain

in the front seat of a Civic parked behind Turtle's,
playing air guitar and wishing for someone to make out with.
          Still. There's music in it.
You know the end: halfway across, scorpion stings frog.

Frog says, "What the fuck? Now we both die."
Scorpion says, "Can't help it, I'm a scorpion."

Tell me again what you will say when I am gone. I am gone already.

Dear First Lover Dear Former Friend Dear Fuck Off

We spent our allotted three years tangled together underneath a soundtrack of hair metal and self-pity, caught between the capital letters of My Family's Hypocrisy and Your Mother's Bad Taste in Second Husbands, between God Hurry Up Already and We Are Already Older Than We Were Yesterday. You said you didn't want to ruin a good friendship, but what choice did we have once I gave myself to the crowd of you, the mouth and roar and tongue and skin of you, the overpriced ticket of you, the Yes I Want You Too of you. The ballads mean proceed with caution. The drum solo means stop. The guitar solo means we are each guilty of failing to consider precisely how the other one will remember these concerts. Listen carefully to a million songs, you'll understand why it's pandering to start with the chorus. For fuck's sake, we should ask more of ourselves.

Elegy for a White Linen Jacket with the Sleeves Shoved Up

We are all smugglers in this decade—
chasing suitcases of money
to rid ourselves of weightier baggage.

Every once in a while something happens that changes
the way the world sees color—

everything that came before so humdrum, so lacking in neon.

I am fifteen and this jacket is from a thrift store
and it is three years too late
but I don't care—

the challenge was always going to be keeping the heroes
as cool as the bad guys,

but it seems there's a formula for our desire to be wanted,

it's no more complicated than removing red from the palette
and turning up the volume on the music.
The violence was fake,
the mysteries easy to solve,

but the hunger—the hunger was always real.

Seven Stories About Fire

1.
Prometheus was trying
to invent the guitar solo.
Fire was his first draft.

2.
The driveway burns—
blaze set by strangers
or neighbors,
a message
or a dare.
Love letter.
Accident.

3.
Everyone gathers to watch
the house go down.
Faces glow
in the heat
of someone
else's tragedy.

4.
On Sunday mornings we are warned
burning is the wages of skin.
Our flesh warms
at the promise,
self-fulfilling
prophecy.

5.
My father smokes,
it's going to kill him,

nothing any of us can do
about it, can't even complain.
Who doesn't crave proximity
to poison; to flame?

6.
You expect a confession
but I was as surprised as anyone
to wake up
on fire.

7.
How about this?
Sometimes I buy cigarettes
and spend the day with them in my pocket,

my body a lie everyone else believes—
on the way home I throw away
the pack unopened, as much power

in letting go as in holding on;
tonight let us crack open our windows
and let out whatever we do not breathe in of each other.

A Hole to the Other Side of the World

Our town is named Love Triangle, named Temporary Housing,
named for a rare flower native to the region

or for the river that divides us. Two dozen churches
and everyone smokes. Across from the old high school

two neighbors lean against a maple
to share a lighter. Each thinks

he is the most bored, alone, frustrated, hungry.
It's football season, which gives them something to talk about.

One of them grew up here, the other a newcomer.
Though divided by income and ten years apart in age

they would claim something like friendship:
they are married to cousins,

their sons play ball together,
one daughter babysits the other,

they both pretend to believe in God,
find it hard to imagine anyone isn't pretending.

One man goes in to eat,
leaving the other alone

as what's left of the sun wanders
behind the tennis courts. He flexes his fingers,

admires the strength in his arms,
worries about

the bile he's tasting in the mornings, lately.
His garage is full of lumber scraps,

broken tools. Soon
he will find his shovel and resume digging.

Portrait of My Imaginary Girlfriend as Joan Jett

For someone whose name I do not remember inventing,
though naturally you went to a different high school
and I met you in a park while at my dad's for the
weekend

Metal is not a mask. The bangs are not a mask.
You put on makeup in order to sweat it away.
To be on stage is to be alive,
the screams show the world is paying attention.
The hot lights. The steam and sway
and strings under your fingers—every song
a balancing act between loud and louder,
every outfit illustrates a new idea of yourself.
The second-saddest story you ever heard
is about someone's mother
selling her guitar when she got married,
the saddest story is a folk song.
Any folk song. You didn't know you were a rebel
until you ran away. You didn't know
the heart could turn black until you woke up
in a hospital bed. Alone is the only lyric worth singing,
midnight the only hour that burns,
your guitar the only lover that listens.
There is no mask. You are no one's clown.
You are faith in disguise, pride dressed up
in someone else's sin. You are vibration,
you are clean sound picked up, amplified—
the secret is knowing exactly how much distortion
it takes to make a stranger fall in love.

Portrait of Us as a Triple-Necked, Heart-Shaped Electric Guitar

for A., who might not remember

A guitar is a promise to the body,
is water rising toward bridge,
is us lost
on our way somewhere meaningful.
Every time I say *I'm sorry*
you say *I know.*
I'm learning to say *I apologize* instead—
this is the legacy of us,
it's what I'll be thinking about years later
when I watch you on *Jeopardy!*
plus of course your mouth
in the form of a question.
Sometimes the show
matters more than the music.
Sometimes a guitar has to make a statement.
At least we love the same songs
unless one of us is pretending.
A guitar is catalyst, is climax,
is compromise between form and function,
is us breathing life into each other
and into this moment we might both forget:
it's summer. It's raining.
We're driving aimlessly,
fast-forwarding to the ballads.
You're holding my hand.

Alternative Uses for Guitar Pick Snagged at a Bon Jovi Concert in 1986

Ineffective monocle. Ill-fitting bottle cap.
Lint remover. Slow comb.

Badge of honor. Down payment. Souvenir
from a year

everyone would rather forget.
Patch for that rip in the screen door.

Bowl of tears. Ninja star.
Paper football.

Bandage to hold together the ragged edges
of my parents' marriage. Lighter for cigarettes

stolen from purse, pocket, bedside table.
Sex toy.

Butter knife.
Petal on a wet, black drumstick.

Planchette dragging
across the letters of my name,

erasing as it goes.

How Things Turned Out

What salt does to flesh, what water, what famine—
the tales time tells about the body, and always
the same ending. Our faith
in storytelling is misplaced. I have not
considered Brian King in years, until today
when I learned across a vast distance
that his corpse washed onto the wan sands
of Gulf Shores, three weeks after he vanished
while out fishing alone. Three weeks
of wind and soak and brine and bloat: such destruction
wrought on the soft shell of a life. Brian King was forty-five,
father of three, divorced, and in the obituary photo,
jowly and bald, as if a middle-aged man
had swallowed the second baseman
from my Pony League team who was all whip-arm
and wheels, a threat to steal on every pitch.
I am forty-five. My body is not what it was. Nor,
mercifully, what it will be. In the movie version
of my life, I age like Redford, all close-up
and soft focus and golden-hued wheat fields
to halo my beauty lines. No room for drowning,
no middle-age vacation derailed by death,
this narrative destined for three full acts.
I have a Brian King story, though perhaps not one
I should be telling. There is no lesson in it. We are fifteen
and practice has ended for the Dodgers
or maybe we are the Cubs that season. Sweaty
and adrenaline-buzzed, we cross the wooden bridge
that spans the river and divides the park into itself
and he says, "Do you want me to suck your dick?"
I'm not sure how honest I'm being if I say
now that I was tempted then, or curious,
consumed by the various cravings of skin,

but what I say to him is, "No, I'm good,"
and he says, "Shut up," and calls me a name.
We never speak of it again, nor of much else,
and then we threw our flat hats into the humidity
over the football field. I moved away, he became
a cop in our hometown, and eventually, I now know,
he divorced and died. How things turned out
is the only way they ever will. Burning
in his lungs, sudden stillness of his limbs;
the heart, the heart, the heart holding on. Perhaps
if I'd said yes on the bridge, he would have
punched me until my nose bled.
Perhaps it would've gone another way.

Elegy for Where I Was Born

I have often said I was born on a houseboat anchored
                along a grassy bank under
a willow near where the river bends
        like a missing man's elbow. So much green. Rain,
or the promise of rain. My mother's hair a dark tent. Her face
      bent to mine. Her body my bread.
                The crows arranged
on the roof, just so, all silhouette and contrast—this is
                how I remember it,
      as if such a moment could last. As if, even then,
    I could have seen it from every angle. As if anyone
has ever seen such stillness. As if to see is anything
         like to understand.
    To love a place is to leave it behind before
              it ceases to exist.

NOTES

"I Have Harnessed Myself Ridiculously to a House Three Miles Outside a Small Town in Alabama" is after Lucy Brock-Broido.

"Everything I Know About Life I Learned from 1980s Action Shows" is after Jeanine Hall Gailey.

"Cigarette vs. Cookie" is after Karen Skolfield.

The title "How to Set a Fire and Why" is borrowed from Jesse Ball.

"What Religion Means to Me" is after Tony Hoagland.

The first line of "In Praise of Charlotte Giattina's 1988 Monte Carlo SS" is borrowed from Robert Lowell.

The title "There Is No Other Devil Anymore" is a line from Wyslawa Szymborska.

ACKNOWLEDGMENTS

I am grateful to the editors of the journals where many of these poems first appeared, sometimes in a different form or under different title:

2 Bridges Review: "Dear First Lover Dear Former Friend Dear Fuck Off"

The Adroit Journal: "Crimes I Did Not Commit" and "How Things Turned Out"

Apple Valley Review: "A Hole to the Other Side of the World"

Bat City Review: "Ouroboros, Alabama"

Bloodroot Literary Magazine: "Boom Box"

Camroc Press Review: "All Weather Wants to Be Some Other Kind of Weather"

The Chattahoochee Review: "Self-Portrait as C.C. DeVille Auditioning for Poison"

The Collagist: "Portrait of My Father as Tatooine" and "Dungeon Master's Guide to Eighth Grade"

The Country Dog Review: "Still Life"

Daphne Magazine: "Alternative Uses for a Guitar Pick Snagged at a Bon Jovi Concert in 1986"

The Ellis Review: "Elegy for Where I Was Born"

Epiphany: "Self-Portrait as Dustin Hoffman in *Tootsie*"

FRiGG: "The Older Brother's Guide to Cheating at Monopoly"

Gravel: "Elegy for a White Linen Jacket with the Sleeves Shoved Up"

Hayden's Ferry Review: "Happy Hollow Road, 1960-1979: A History in Six Voices"

Hermeneutic Chaos: "Portrait of Us as a Triple-Necked, Heart-Shaped Electric Guitar"

Heron Tree: "I Have Harnessed Myself Ridiculously to a House Three Miles Outside a Small Town in Alabama"

Hobart: "The Fathers at the Little League Field"

Hobble Creek Review: "The Existence of Han Solo Explains the Universe"

The MacGuffin: "The Boys in the Parking Lot"

miPOEsias: "Rescue"

The Mondegreen: "Ever Since the Movies Taught Me About the Space-Time Continuum"

Moon City Review: "In Praise of Charlotte Giattina's 1988 Monte Carlo SS"

New South: "How I Got This Way"

Peninsula Poets: "The Skies Above the Little League Fields of My Memory"

The Pinch: "Land Fall"

Radar Poetry: "Self-Portrait Following a Trail of Reese's Pieces"

Rattle: "What Religion Means to Me"

REAL: Regarding Arts and Letters: "Seven Postcards from Trussville, Alabama" and "Dead Man's Float"

Red Earth Review: "Cigarette vs. Cookie" and "The Boy Who Believed in the Girl Who Did Not Believe in God"

Reed: "To All the Boys Who Died Before Graduation"

Split Lip: "Everything I Know About Life I Learned from 1980s Action Shows"

Spry Literary Journal: "Portrait of My Imaginary Girlfriend as Joan Jett"

Then and If: "The Elegy Arrives Too Late to Change Anything, Which Is Sort of the Definition of Elegy"

Tupelo Quarterly: "Portrait of My Brother as Indiana Jones"

Wherewithal: "Elegy for *Dirty Dancing*"

ABOUT THE AUTHOR

Amorak Huey is author of two previous poetry collections: *Seducing the Asparagus Queen* (Cloudbank Books, 2018), winner of the Vern Rutsala Prize; and *Ha Ha Ha Thump* (Sundress Publications, 2015). Co-author of the textbook *Poetry: A Writers' Guide and Anthology* (Bloomsbury Academic, 2018), he teaches writing at Grand Valley State University in Michigan.

OTHER SUNDRESS TITLES

Arabilis
Leah Silvieus
$16

Match Cut
Letitia Trent
$16

Passing Through Humansville
Karen Craigo
$16

Phantom Tongue
Steven Sanchez
$15

Citizens of the Mausoleum
Rodney Gomez
$15

Hands That Break and Scar
Sarah A. Chavez
$15

Before Isadore
Shannon Elizabeth Hardwick
$15

They Were Bears
Sarah Marcus
$15

Afakasi | Half-Caste
Hali F. Sofala-Jones
$16

Marvels
MR Sheffield
$20

Divining Bones
Charlie Bondus
$16

The Minor Territories
Danielle Sellers
$15

Actual Miles
Jim Warner
$15

Either Way, You're Done
Stephanie McCarley Dugger
$15

Big Thicket Blues
Natalie Giarratano
$15

At Whatever Front
Les Kay
$15

www.ingramcontent.com/pod-product-compliance
Lightning Source LLC
Chambersburg PA
CBHW031148090426
42738CB00008B/1262